T0130350

# Shopping at The Farm Shop

**Coloured Version**

Children Saving our Planet Series

**CAROL SUTTERS**

Illustrated by William Fong

*© 2021 CAROL SUTTERS. All rights reserved.*

*No part of this book may be reproduced, stored in a retrieval system, or transmitted by any means without the written permission of the author.*

*AuthorHouse™ UK*
*1663 Liberty Drive*
*Bloomington, IN 47403 USA*
*www.authorhouse.co.uk*
*UK TFN: 0800 0148641 (Toll Free inside the UK)*
*UK Local: 02036 956322 (+44 20 3695 6322 from outside the UK)*

*Because of the dynamic nature of the Internet, any web addresses or links contained in this book may have changed since publication and may no longer be valid. The views expressed in this work are solely those of the author and do not necessarily reflect the views of the publisher, and the publisher hereby disclaims any responsibility for them.*

*Any people depicted in stock imagery provided by Getty Images are models, and such images are being used for illustrative purposes only.*
*Certain stock imagery © Getty Images.*

*This book is printed on acid-free paper.*

*ISBN: 978-1-6655-8640-5 (sc)*
*ISBN: 978-1-6655-8641-2 (e)*

*Library of Congress Control Number: 2021903690*

*Print information available on the last page.*

*Published by AuthorHouse 04/15/2021*

authorHOUSE®

Today Katie and Tom will go to the local shop with their Mum. As they travel down the road on their scooters Mum remarks, "*We can walk there as we are going to the Farm Shop to support the local farmer.*

Farm Shop

*We can just buy what food we need and not excess to our needs. It is estimated that one third of all food produced in the UK ends up wasted. This amounts to about 7 million tons of food each year. It is a waste of food and energy, including making unnecessary carbon emissions. Waste food is dumped in landfill sites where it rots and becomes a significant source of methane, a potent greenhouse gas."*

SALE
FRUITS & VEG

Mum continues, "*The farm shop sells produce like fruit and vegetables grown on farms in the local village. It also sells meat reared locally. Other local producers can sell cheese, jams, bread and cakes there. It was found that food bought in local farm shops is sometimes cheaper than food from supermarkets, which may have been transported many hundreds of miles from other countries. Buying locally is called cutting food miles and it cuts down carbon transportation emissions. Additionally, farm shop produce is guaranteed to be fresh.*"

Mum requests to the farmer's wife, "*We want to buy a cauliflower, some potatoes, carrots and tomatoes.*" Tom asks, "*Please can we also have some green peas in their pods as I like them?*"

ORGANIC
VEGETABLES

Kate says, "*What does that mean? The sign saying these vegetables are grown organically?*"

The farmer's wife replies, "*We grow the vegetables on the farm without using fertilisers which kill pests that eat the crop. Besides pests that eat the crops there are slugs, worms and other insects in the soil and in the air which are beneficial. We do not want to kill them as they occur naturally and help create good soil for the crops in the field to thrive.*"

The farmer's wife continues, "*If we use fertilisers to prevent the crops being eaten by pests, that will give us better crops to sell and make profit but there are other problems with using fertiliser. Fertilisers contain nitrogen which forms nitrates. If too much fertiliser is used, the excess nitrates can be washed away into rivers with rainwater and can enter our drink water systems. If excess nitrates get into our drinking water, this can make humans ill.*"

She continues, "*High concentrations of nitrate pollutants can also be harmful to the fish and plants in the local rivers. Nitrates promote excessive growth of algae which reduce the oxygen in the water and also cause fish to die. Plants and animals living in harmony together in these ponds and water systems is an example of an ecosystem. Nitrates can harm marine ecosystems.*"

Mum remarks, "*We need to find a way to grow plants and vegetables for us to eat that does not harm our environment or humans at the same time.*"

The farmer's wife comments, "*This can be done on a farm by certain crop rotations and other farming methods. If farmers grow crops organically, they use natural methods such as compost for fertiliser, which does not contain added chemicals or manufactured fertilisers. They also use natural seeds which have not been modified by scientists. In the past, some farmers undertook Intensive farming using lots of fertiliser without regard for the environment. They were just concerned with making as much profit as possible.*"

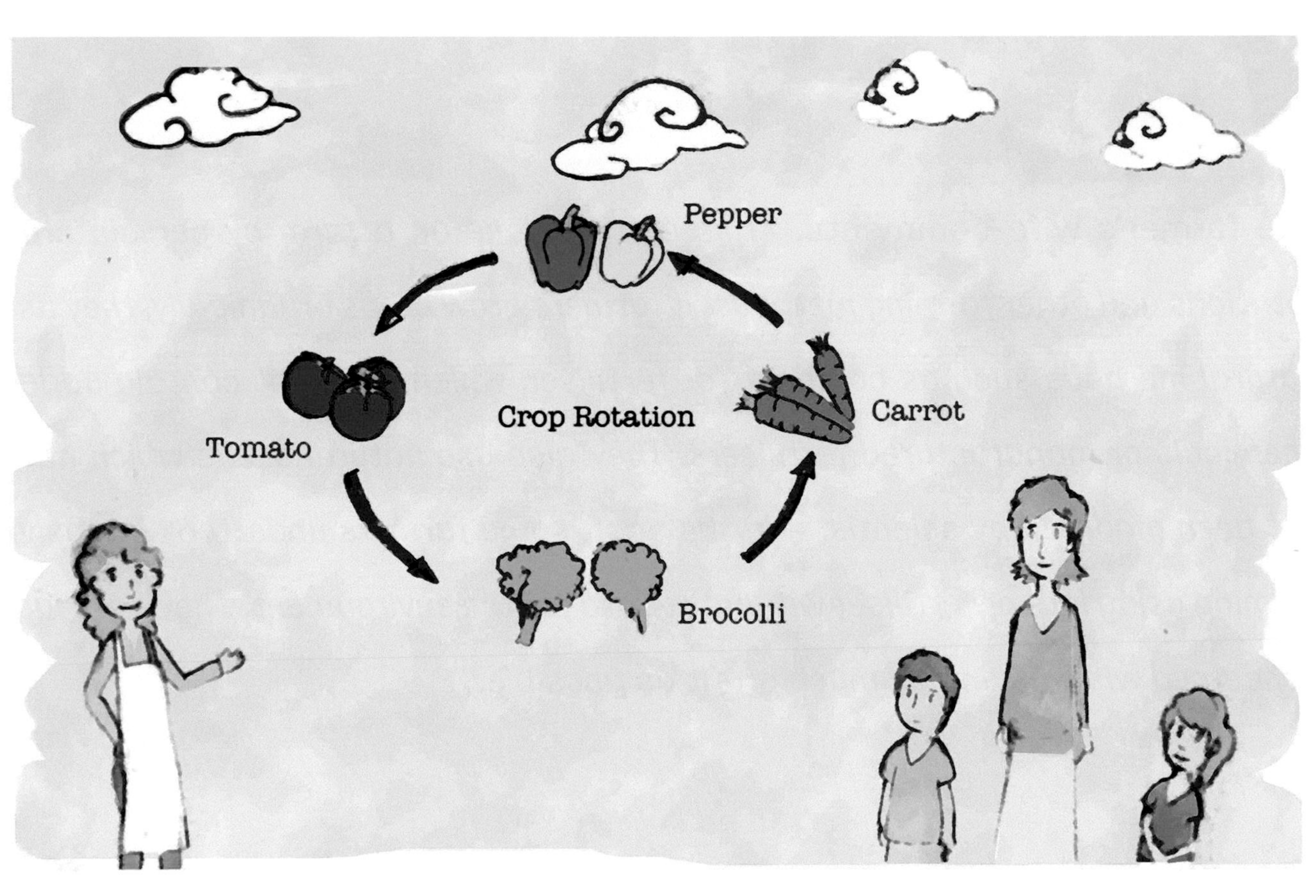
Pepper
Crop Rotation
Tomato
Carrot
Brocolli

The farmer's wife continues, *"But, we are now changing to organic farming to preserve the earth and animals. We need to grow enough food to feed us all without destroying the biodiverse ecosystems on earth."*

FARM SHOP

Kate asks, *"Can you buy lots of different types of organic foods?"*

Organic Fruits and Veg

*"Yes" says Mum.*

*"Let's play a game for you to guess?"*

*"Can you buy organic yoghurt?" – "Yes."*

*"Organic milk?" – "Yes."*

*"Organic strawberries?" – "Yes."*

*"Organic lettuces?" – "Yes."*

*"Organic cooked cakes?" –"Yes."*

*"Organic bread?" – "Yes."*

*"Organic beef?" – "Yes."*

*"Organic cereal?"- "Yes."*

Mum reports, "*Farmers are trying to produce enough food for us all to eat across the world. But it is a balance between having suitably rich soil, enough water, correct climate and not destroying the soil and ecosystems. We do not want to cause harm in order to grow crops in fields.*"

*“An alternative approach becoming popular is growing crops without using soil. Crops such as tomatoes, peppers, cucumbers, flowers and others can be grown. The roots of these crops can be suspended in gravel and exposed to oxygen, and a nutritious food such as duck manure or fish excrement. This system has the advantage of using less water and we can grow these plants in greenhouses and so not use precious land, which can be left to nature. The system is called hydrophonics.”*

On their departure Mum suggests, *“We will talk about a few ecosystems to explain this to you when we return home.”*

**What did we learn today? (tick the box if you understood and agree)**

☐ Farm shops sell fresh meat reared locally and fruit and vegetables grown locally. Buying there avoids using fossil fuels for transportation of food from distant countries that cause pollution. It also supports home grown producers.

☐ Fertilisers can increase the amount of crops we harvest but their excessive use can cause damage to local ecosystems and our drinking water.

☐ Farmers need to re-examine the way we farm our fruit and vegetables so that we can use less fertilisers which drain into nearby rivers and damage the plants and animals living there.

☐ Sometimes, it is possible to grow certain crops together or in rotation in fields to prevent pests destroying the fruit and food.

☐ Crops can be grown without soil which gives us an alternative way to produce food without destroying forests for land use.

☐ Fish and water plants live in harmony in natural streams and this is an example of an ecosystem.

*Find out about Kate and Tom's Holiday by the Sea in book 8.*

# Children Saving our Planet Series

Books

1. Tom and Kate Go to Westminster
2. Kate and Tom Learn About Fossil Fuels
3. Tom and Kate Chose Green Carbon
4. Tress and Deforestation
5. Our Neighbourhood Houses
6. Our Neighbourhood Roads
7. Shopping at the Farm Shop
8. Travelling to a Holiday by the Sea
9. Picnic at the Seaside on Holiday

**10. The Oceans and Coral**

**11. Our Carbon Footprint**

**12. Fire Fire**

**13. The Antarctic Warms Up**

**14. The Canada Catastrophe**

**15. The Coronavirus and saving the Planet**

**16. The Children's Rebellion and Climate Change**

These series of simple books explain the landmark importance of Children's participation in the Extinction rebellion protest. Children actively want to encourage and support adults to urgently tackle both the Climate and the Biodiversity emergencies. The booklets enable children at an early age to understand some of the scientific principles that are affecting the destruction of the planet. If global political and economic systems fail to address the climate emergency, the responsibility will rest upon children to save the Planet for themselves.

*This series is dedicated to*

*Theodore, Aria and Ophelia.*

Printed in the United States
by Baker & Taylor Publisher Services

Printed in the United States
by Baker & Taylor Publisher Services